D1714703

Contents

Introduction

Pickleball is one of the fastest-growing sports in the world, blending elements from tennis, badminton, and ping pong into a dynamic, fast-paced game that players of all ages and skill levels can enjoy. With a low barrier to entry and a strong emphasis on skill, strategy, and precision, pickleball offers something for everyone—whether you're looking for a fun social game or an intense competitive match.

What is Pickleball?

Pickleball is a paddle sport played on a badminton-sized court with a slightly modified tennis net. The game can be played as singles (one-on-one) or doubles (two-on-two). The objective is simple: use a paddle to hit a plastic ball with holes (similar to a wiffle ball) over the net and into your opponent's court, with the goal of scoring points by forcing errors or faults from the opposing side.

The game is designed to be accessible for players of all skill levels, making it a sport that can be played recreationally or competitively at any age. With easy-to-learn rules and engaging play, pickleball has quickly become a favorite in communities, schools, and even professional sports circuits worldwide.

History of the Sport

Pickleball was invented in 1965 by three friends—Joel Pritchard, Bill Bell, and Barney McCallum—on Bainbridge Island, Washington. The story goes that Pritchard and Bell were trying to find a way to entertain their families with an outdoor game but didn't have the proper equipment for badminton. They improvised with ping pong paddles and a wiffle ball, lowering the badminton net, and setting up a makeshift court in Pritchard's backyard. The game quickly caught on, and over time, it evolved into the sport we know today.

The quirky name "pickleball" is often attributed to the Pritchard family's dog, "Pickles," who would cha after stray balls during games. Another version of the story suggests the name was inspired by the "pickle boat," a term from rowing where leftover crew members formed a team—much like how the sport itself was a mix of different games.

Popularity and Growth Worldwide

What started as a backyard game has exploded into a global phenomenon. Today, pickleball is played i countries all over the world, with millions of players in the United States, Canada, and beyond. One of the key drivers of the sport's growth is its accessibility—pickleball courts are easy to set up, and the equipment required is minimal, making it an ideal game for community centers, schools, and recreational parks.

In recent years, the sport has gained even more traction due to the formation of professional leagues and tournaments, including the USA Pickleball National Championships and the Major League Pickleba (MLP). With celebrity endorsements and sponsorships from major sports brands, the sport is becomin staple in both casual and professional sports communities. Players from other racket sports like tennis and badminton are also picking up pickleball to enhance their skills and stay competitive in a new, challenging format.

Benefits of Playing Pickleball

Pickleball offers numerous benefits, both physical and social. Here are just a few reasons why players are falling in love with the sport:

1. **Physical Health**: Pickleball provides a great cardiovascular workout, helping to improve endurance, agility, and hand-eye coordination. The game also promotes full-body movement, as players must engage their legs, core, and arms during gameplay.

2. **Mental Health**: The strategic elements of pickleball encourage mental sharpness and quick decision-making. It helps improve focus, concentration, and problem-solving skills on the court. The social aspect also contributes to positive mental well-being, providing opportunities for players to interact, laugh, and enjoy friendly competition.

3. **Accessibility**: One of the best things about pickleball is that it can be played by people of all ages and fitness levels. The smaller court size and lighter ball mean that players don't need the same level of speed and power required for other racket sports like tennis. This makes it a great option for families, seniors, and players looking for a low-impact activity.

4. **Community**: Pickleball fosters a strong sense of community. Whether you're playing at your local park or joining a competitive league, the sport encourages camaraderie, teamwork, and sportsmanship. Pickleball enthusiasts often talk about how welcoming and supportive the pickleball community is, offering newcomers a chance to connect and make friends easily.

Chapter 1: The Rules of Pickleball

Pickleball has straightforward rules that are easy to learn but essential to master for competitive play. Understanding these rules will not only keep the game fair but also allow players to focus on improving their skills and strategy.

Basic Setup

Pickleball is played on a rectangular court that measures 20 feet wide and 44 feet long, the same dimensions as a doubles badminton court. The court is divided into two equal sides by a net that stands inches high at the sidelines and 34 inches high in the center. The game can be played either as singles doubles, with the same court size used for both formats.

- **Court Layout**: The court is divided into several key areas:

    o **The Baseline**: The back boundary line of the court.

    o **The Sidelines**: The side boundaries of the court.

    o **The Non-Volley Zone (Kitchen)**: A 7-foot area on either side of the net where players are not allowed to hit volleys. More on the kitchen rules later.

    o **The Service Area**: Each side of the court is divided into left and right service areas, which are used to determine where the serve must land.

- **Equipment**:

- Paddles: Players use paddles made of wood, composite, or graphite. Paddles are larger than ping pong paddles but smaller than tennis rackets.
- Pickleball: The ball is made of hard plastic with holes, resembling a wiffle ball. The ball comes in different colors, with yellow and white being the most common.

Scoring System

Understanding how points are scored is crucial for winning a pickleball game. The rules for scoring differ slightly between singles and doubles matches.

- **How to Score**:
  - Only the serving team can score points. A point is earned when the opposing team commits a fault, such as hitting the ball out of bounds or failing to return the ball over the net.
  - Games are typically played to 11 points, and a team must win by 2 points. In more competitive settings, games may be played to 15 or 21 points.

- **Winning the Game**:
  - In both singles and doubles play, a player or team must reach 11 points and be at least points ahead of the opponent to win.
  - For example, if the score is 10-10, the game continues until one player or team leads by 2 points, such as 12-10 or 13-11.

Serve and Serve Receive

The serve is one of the most critical aspects of the game and has specific rules that must be followed. A strong, accurate serve can set the tone for the entire rally.

- **Proper Serving Technique**:
  - The serve must be executed with an underhand motion, with the paddle contacting the ball below the server's waist.
  - The server must stand behind the baseline and serve diagonally to the opponent's service area.
  - The serve must clear the net and land within the correct service area (not in the non-volley zone).

- **Faults and Violations**:
  - A fault occurs if the server fails to serve the ball into the diagonal service court or if the ball lands in the kitchen. If a fault occurs, the serve is lost to the other team in doubles or the serve switches to the opponent in singles.
  - A "let" occurs when the serve hits the net but still lands in the correct service area. In this case, the serve is redone.

- **Double-Bounce Rule**:
  - After the serve, both teams must let the ball bounce once before hitting it. This rule ensures that neither team can rush the net for a quick volley after the serve. Once the ball has bounced once on each side, volleys are permitted.

The Non-Volley Zone (Kitchen)

The kitchen, or non-volley zone, is one of the most unique and important aspects of pickleball. This area extends 7 feet from the net on both sides and restricts players from volleying the ball while standing inside it.

- **Understanding the Kitchen Rules**:
  - Players are not allowed to hit a volley (a shot hit before the ball bounces) while standing inside or stepping into the kitchen.
  - Players can enter the kitchen to hit a ball after it bounces but must exit before attempting to volley another ball.

- **Key Violations**:
  - A player commits a fault if they volley the ball while standing in the kitchen or if their momentum causes them to step into the kitchen after a volley.
  - It's important to stay aware of foot placement, as even touching the kitchen line while volleying results in a fault.

Singles vs. Doubles Rules

While many rules are shared between singles and doubles, there are some important distinctions, especially regarding the serve and court coverage.

- **Court Coverage**:
  - In singles, players are responsible for covering the entire court by themselves, which requires quick movement and smart shot placement.
  - In doubles, each team member is responsible for half the court, allowing for more specialized roles and coordinated strategy.

- **Serve Rotation (Doubles Play)**:
  - In doubles, each team has two serves per service turn—one for each player. When a fault is made, the serve passes to the partner. If both players have lost their serve, the serve then goes to the opposing team.
  - In singles, the serve alternates between players after each fault or point.

- **Positioning and Movement**:

- In doubles, players often start side by side, each covering half of the court. As the rally progresses, positioning may change, with one player moving forward to the kitchen line and the other covering the backcourt.
- In singles, players constantly shift positions to cover the entire court, making footwork and anticipation vital.

By mastering these fundamental rules, players can ensure they are playing within the guidelines and avoid committing costly faults. This knowledge also lays the foundation for developing more advanced strategies, which will be covered in later chapters.

Chapter 2: Mastering Pickleball Techniques

Pickleball might be easy to learn, but mastering its various techniques takes practice and attention to detail. In this chapter, we will dive into the fundamental and advanced techniques that every player should know to improve their game. Whether you are playing singles or doubles, these skills will help you gain an edge over your opponents.

Grips and Stances

The way you hold your paddle and position yourself on the court can significantly affect your performance. Having a solid grip and proper stance will allow for more control, power, and precision in your shots.

- **How to Hold the Paddle**:
  - The most common and recommended way to hold the paddle is with a **continental grip**. To achieve this, hold the paddle as if you are shaking hands with it. This grip is versatile and works well for both forehand and backhand shots, allowing for quick transitions between the two.

- **Different Grip Types**:
  - **Continental Grip**: This is the go-to grip for most players because of its versatility. It allows you to hit forehand, backhand, volleys, and overhead shots without needing to switch grips during a rally.
  - **Eastern Forehand Grip**: This grip is useful for players who want more power in their forehand shots. It's similar to how you would hold a tennis racket for a forehand stroke.
  - **Western Grip**: This grip is less common in pickleball but can generate additional topspin on your forehand shots. However, it is harder to transition to a backhand with this grip.

- **Stance**:
  - **Ready Position**: Keep your feet shoulder-width apart, knees slightly bent, and weight balanced on the balls of your feet. Hold the paddle in front of you at chest height, ready to react quickly to incoming shots.

- o **Footwork**: Good footwork is key to positioning yourself for success. Stay light on your feet and ready to move laterally or forward and backward. Always step into your shots rather than reaching, as this will improve your balance and accuracy.

Basic Shots

Mastering the basic shots is crucial for consistent play. Each type of shot has a specific use depending on your position on the court and the situation during a rally.

- **Forehand and Backhand Drive**:
  - o The forehand drive is one of the most powerful and commonly used shots in pickleball. To execute, step into the shot with your front foot, rotate your hips, and swing through the ball with a smooth, controlled motion.
  - o The backhand drive is often more challenging for beginners but equally important. Hold the paddle with your non-dominant side facing the net, and swing from low to high while keeping your wrist firm to generate power.

- **Dinks and Drop Shots**:
  - o The **dink** is a soft, controlled shot that lands in your opponent's non-volley zone (kitchen), forcing them to hit up, which creates an opportunity for you to attack. Dinks are most effective when you are at the kitchen line. To execute a dink, use a gentle upward motion with the paddle and keep the ball low to the net.
  - o A **drop shot** is similar to a dink but is played from the backcourt or midcourt. The goal of the drop shot is to land the ball softly in the opponent's kitchen, making it difficult for them to return the ball with power.

- **The Serve**:
  - o The serve is an underhand stroke that initiates the rally. A good serve can put pressure on your opponent from the start. There are two main types of serves:
    - **High Serve**: This serve is hit deep into the opponent's court with an arc, giving you more time to approach the net. This is effective against opponents who prefer to stay at the baseline.
    - **Low Serve**: This serve is hit low and fast, aiming to keep your opponent at the baseline. The goal is to force a weak return that allows you to take control of the rally.

- **The Lob Shot**:
  - o The lob is a high, arcing shot intended to go over your opponent's head, particularly if they are positioned close to the net. This shot can catch an opponent off guard and force them to retreat. However, it must be executed with precision; if hit too shallow, it can give your opponent an easy smash.

Advanced Techniques

Once you have mastered the basic shots, you can begin to incorporate more advanced techniques into your game. These techniques require finesse and practice but can give you a significant advantage.

- **The Smash**:
    - A smash is a powerful overhead shot that is usually the result of a poorly executed lob by your opponent. To perform a smash, wait for the ball to rise above your head, then swing down forcefully while keeping your eyes on the ball. The goal is to hit the ball sharply downward, making it difficult for your opponent to return.

- **Spin Shots**:
    - Adding spin to your shots can increase their unpredictability and make them harder to return. There are two types of spins commonly used in pickleball:
        - **Topspin**: To add topspin, brush the paddle upward against the ball. This makes the ball dip quickly after crossing the net, causing it to bounce low.
        - **Backspin**: To add backspin, brush the paddle downward against the ball. This keeps the ball low and can cause it to float or skid after bouncing.

- **The Block Shot**:
    - The block shot is a defensive technique used to counter hard, fast shots from your opponent. Rather than swinging at the ball, you simply use the paddle to "block" the ball, absorbing its energy and guiding it back over the net. This shot is particularly useful when your opponent smashes the ball at you.

- **Resetting the Ball in Defense**:
    - When your opponent is in a strong attacking position, it's important to reset the rally and regain control. To do this, you can use a soft shot that neutralizes your opponent' power. This is often referred to as a **"reset" shot** and is aimed at the opponent's kitchen, forcing them to slow down the pace and reset the point.

Shot Placement and Strategy

Understanding where and when to place your shots is key to developing a strategic approach to the game. Mastering shot placement can give you an edge over your opponents by keeping them off-balance and forcing errors.

- **Hitting to the Backcourt**: A well-placed deep shot to the backcourt can push your opponent away from the net, giving you time to move into a more aggressive position. This is especially useful when you are on the defensive and need to reset the rally.

- **Targeting Weak Spots**: Pay attention to your opponent's weaknesses, such as poor backhand technique or slower reaction time on one side of the court. Focus on hitting to those areas to force mistakes.

- **Mixing Up Shots**: A successful pickleball player is unpredictable. Alternate between soft shots like dinks and harder shots like drives and smashes to keep your opponent guessing. This variation in shot selection will make it harder for your opponent to settle into a rhythm.

onclusion of Chapter 2

 this chapter, we've covered the essential techniques that form the foundation of successful pickleball ay. By mastering basic shots like the forehand, backhand, and dink, while also incorporating advanced chniques like spin shots and smashes, you'll be well on your way to becoming a more versatile and fective player.

emember, consistent practice of these skills is key to improving your game. Whether you're just arting out or looking to sharpen your competitive edge, dedicating time to these techniques will give u a strong advantage in both singles and doubles play.

hapter 3: Singles Play Strategies

ngles pickleball is a fast-paced, demanding game that requires sharp strategic thinking, quick footwork, d a deep understanding of court positioning. Unlike doubles, where the court is shared with a partner, ngles play forces you to cover the entire court, making it essential to develop strategies that maximize ur strengths and exploit your opponent's weaknesses.

 this chapter, we will explore the strategies that will help you dominate the singles court, from anaging court space and shot selection to defensive and offensive techniques.

urt Positioning

 singles pickleball, proper court positioning is the foundation for effective play. Because you're sponsible for covering the entire court, positioning yourself wisely will reduce the amount of running u need to do while keeping you in control of the game.

- **Managing Court Space**:
  - The first rule of singles play is to always stay centered on the court as much as possible. By staying close to the middle, you minimize the distance you need to move to return shots, whether they are sent to your forehand or backhand side.
  - After serving, move quickly to the center of the court just behind the baseline. This positioning will allow you to cover both angles of return and give you more time to react to your opponent's shot.

- **Dominating the Centerline**:

- In singles, controlling the centerline of the court is key. By maintaining a central position, you force your opponent to hit wide or deep, increasing the likelihood that they will make an error. The closer you are to the centerline, the easier it is to defend both sides of the court.
- The centerline also gives you the shortest path to any part of the court, allowing you to cover ground more efficiently.

Shot Selection

Smart shot selection is critical to winning in singles. In this section, we'll explore the different types of shots that are most effective in singles play and when to use them.

- **Hitting to the Backcourt**:
  - In singles, hitting deep shots to your opponent's backcourt is a key strategy. By forcing your opponent to retreat toward the baseline, you not only gain control of the net but also give yourself more time to react to their return.
  - Deep shots are especially useful when your opponent is approaching the kitchen line. A well-placed drive to the backcourt can disrupt their position and create opportunities for you to dictate the pace of the rally.

- **When to Use Dinks and Drives**:
  - Dinking is less common in singles than in doubles because it requires getting close to the net, which can leave you vulnerable to lobs or passing shots. However, well-executed dinks can still be effective in singles if used sparingly and strategically.
  - Drives, on the other hand, are often the go-to shot in singles play. The fast pace of a drive shot can catch your opponent off-guard, especially if they are positioned far back in the court. By mixing deep drives with softer shots like dinks or drop shots, you can keep your opponent guessing and prevent them from settling into a rhythm.

Defensive Play

Defense in singles is about staying composed, managing the court, and anticipating your opponent's next move. Here are some key defensive strategies that will help you stay in control, even when your opponent is on the attack.

- **Controlling the Kitchen Line**:
  - Although dinking is less prevalent in singles, controlling the kitchen line is still important. If your opponent tries to move toward the kitchen and dink or drop-shot you, maintaining your position just behind the kitchen line can force them to hit up on the ball, giving you the opportunity to attack.
  - The key to kitchen defense in singles is balance. If you are drawn into the kitchen, be prepared to quickly retreat to the baseline if your opponent attempts a lob shot over

your head. Footwork and anticipation are crucial in transitioning between the kitchen and baseline.

- **Managing Opponent's Angles**:
  - One of the biggest challenges in singles is managing the angles your opponent creates, especially during crosscourt shots. To minimize this threat, aim to hit more straight shots (down the line) instead of giving your opponent opportunities to angle you off the court.
  - Keep your shots deep and down the middle when possible. This reduces the angle your opponent can create, making it harder for them to hit sharp crosscourt winners. By limiting their options, you can force errors and take control of the point.

ffensive Play

win in singles, you need to seize every opportunity to go on the offensive. The following offensive rategies will help you put pressure on your opponent and create scoring opportunities.

- **Attacking with Speed and Precision**:
  - In singles, speed and precision are two of your greatest assets. Well-timed, powerful shots can push your opponent back and force them into uncomfortable positions. However, it's important to balance power with precision. Wild, uncontrolled shots will likely go out of bounds or hit the net, so focus on hitting hard while still aiming for deep corners or sidelines.
  - When you see an opportunity, approach the net with a combination of speed and finesse. Once at the net, control the rally with quick volleys and sharp angles that leave your opponent scrambling to recover.

- **Exploiting Opponent Weaknesses**:
  - Every player has weaknesses, whether it's a weaker backhand, slow footwork, or difficulty hitting overhead shots. Early in the game, observe your opponent's tendencies and weaknesses, then craft your strategy around exploiting them.
  - For example, if your opponent struggles with backhand returns, direct most of your shots to that side. If they are slow to move laterally, hit wider shots that stretch them out. By continually targeting their weaknesses, you increase the chance of forcing errors and capitalizing on scoring opportunities.

veloping a Game Plan

singles pickleball, a solid game plan is essential for success. Your game plan should be adaptable and sed on the type of player you are facing, the conditions of the court, and your own strengths and eaknesses.

- **Assessing Your Opponent**:
  - The first step in creating a game plan is assessing your opponent's style of play. Are they aggressive, always looking for the opportunity to rush the net? Or do they prefer to play defensively, staying back at the baseline? Understanding their tendencies will allow you to adjust your strategy accordingly.
  - If you're facing an aggressive player, it may be wise to slow the game down with more soft shots, drop shots, and dinks, forcing them to be patient. Against defensive players, you'll want to take more control, hitting deeper shots and rushing the net when possible.

- **Adjusting Mid-Game**:
  - No game plan is perfect, and there will always be moments where you need to adapt on the fly. If your original strategy isn't working, don't be afraid to make adjustments during the match. This could mean switching to more aggressive play, changing the type of shots you're using, or altering your positioning on the court.
  - Pay close attention to how your opponent responds to different types of shots and tactics. If something works, stick with it. If not, pivot quickly to keep your opponent off balance.

Fitness and Conditioning for Singles

Unlike doubles, singles pickleball demands more physical fitness and endurance due to the larger court area you must cover alone. Here are a few fitness and conditioning tips to keep you agile and quick during singles play:

- **Footwork Drills**:
  - Quick, efficient footwork is essential for covering the court in singles. Incorporate footwork drills into your practice sessions to improve your lateral movement, speed, and balance. For example, practice side-shuffles, crossover steps, and quick sprints from baseline to net.

- **Endurance Training**:
  - Singles matches can be physically demanding, especially if they go on for extended periods. Incorporate endurance training into your routine, such as jogging, sprinting, or high-intensity interval training (HIIT), to build the stamina necessary to outlast your opponents.

Conclusion of Chapter 3

Singles pickleball is a game of precision, strategy, and endurance. By mastering court positioning, shot selection, and offensive and defensive techniques, you will gain the tools necessary to dominate the

ngles court. Keep refining your game plan, adapting to your opponent, and improving your fitness
vel, and you'll be well on your way to becoming a top singles player.

Chapter 4: Doubles Play Strategies

Doubles pickleball requires a unique set of strategies compared to singles play. In doubles, teamwork,
ommunication, and coordination are key elements that determine success. Effective doubles play
volves not only individual skills but also how well you and your partner function as a unit. In this
apter, we will explore the essential strategies for doubles play, from proper court positioning and
ovement to advanced tactics like stacking and poaching.

ommunication and Teamwork

ommunication is the foundation of successful doubles play. With two players on the court, it's essential
be in constant communication with your partner to ensure you are both in the right position and
ecuting the correct strategies.

- **How to Talk to Your Partner**:
  - Clear and concise communication with your partner is crucial during the game. Use
    simple verbal cues such as "Mine," "Yours," or "Switch" to avoid confusion during
    rallies. Establish a set of signals or code words before the game to communicate your
    intentions without hesitation.
  - In addition to in-game communication, it's important to talk strategy before and after
    each rally. For example, discuss your plan for the upcoming serve or decide who will
    take the next shot if your opponents hit down the middle.
- **Backing Each Other Up**:
  - In doubles, it's important to work as a team to cover the court. If your partner is pulled
    out of position, you should immediately shift to cover their side. This requires constant
    awareness of both your partner's position and the direction of the ball.
  - In situations where your partner is drawn to one side of the court, such as chasing down
    a wide shot, you need to step in and cover the center of the court to prevent your
    opponents from hitting a winner.

urt Positioning

urt positioning is one of the most important aspects of doubles pickleball. Knowing where to stand
d how to move as a team will give you a significant advantage over your opponents.

- **Splitting the Court: Left-Right and Front-Back Coverage**:

- The most common positioning in doubles is for each player to cover one side of the court (left-right). This division of the court ensures that each player has a defined area of responsibility, making it easier to cover all areas without confusion.

- However, depending on the situation, front-back positioning can also be effective. In this case, one player stays near the kitchen line, while the other remains back near the baseline. This is typically used when returning a deep shot, with the back player defending and the front player ready to attack at the net.

- **The Importance of the Kitchen Line**:

  - In doubles, controlling the kitchen line is crucial. Players who dominate the net area can dictate the pace of the game and apply pressure on their opponents. Both partners should aim to move up to the kitchen line as soon as possible after the serve or return of serve.

  - By staying close to the kitchen line, you can execute dinks, volleys, and quick reflex shots that make it difficult for your opponents to counter. However, you should also be prepared to move back quickly if your opponents attempt a lob shot over your head.

Stacking and Switching

Stacking and switching are advanced positioning strategies that allow players to optimize their strength and put pressure on their opponents.

- **How to Effectively Switch Positions**:

  - Switching refers to the process of trading places with your partner during a rally to maintain optimal positioning. For example, if your partner is drawn to the right side of the court, you should switch to the left side to maintain balance. This ensures that there are no gaps in coverage and keeps both players in play.

  - Good communication is essential for effective switching. Use verbal cues like "Switch" "I got it" to let your partner know when a switch is happening so that neither player is left out of position.

- **Understanding the Advantage of Stacking for Stronger Players**:

  - Stacking is a more advanced tactic often used in doubles to allow the stronger player (e.g., a player with a more dominant forehand) to cover a particular side of the court more consistently. In a traditional doubles setup, each player covers either the left or right side. However, in stacking, both players start on the same side of the court after the serve, then move to their designated positions during the rally.

  - Stacking allows the stronger player to stay on their preferred side, typically covering the forehand side, which often leads to more powerful and consistent shots. It's commonly used by high-level players to maximize their team's strengths.

Dinking in Doubles

The dink is a key shot in doubles pickleball, especially when playing at the kitchen line. Mastering dinking will help you control the pace of the game, forcing your opponents to make mistakes while allowing you to set up more aggressive shots.

- **Dinking Strategies to Force Errors**:
    - Dinking involves hitting a soft shot that lands just over the net in your opponent's kitchen. By keeping the ball low and slow, you limit your opponent's ability to hit hard, forcing them to hit up on the ball. This gives you the opportunity to either continue the soft exchange or set up for a more aggressive attack.
    - The key to effective dinking is patience. Don't try to end the point too early—wait for your opponents to make a mistake, such as hitting the ball too high, and then capitalize on it with a quick volley or smash.

- **Using Crosscourt Dinks to Open Up Opportunities**:
    - Crosscourt dinks are particularly effective in doubles because they force your opponent to move laterally, covering more ground. By hitting your dinks crosscourt, you increase the distance your opponents have to travel, which can lead to errors or weaker returns.
    - Additionally, crosscourt dinks can create angles that open up the court for you and your partner. For example, after hitting a crosscourt dink, your opponent may be forced out of position, leaving gaps that you can exploit with a quick putaway shot.

Poaching

Poaching is an aggressive tactic in doubles that involves one player stepping into their partner's side of the court to intercept and attack a shot. It's a powerful move when timed correctly but requires good communication and anticipation.

- **Knowing When to Poach**:
    - Poaching is most effective when you anticipate a weak return from your opponent. For example, if your opponent is off-balance or forced into a difficult position, you can step across the court and intercept their shot with a powerful volley or smash.
    - However, poaching requires excellent timing and coordination with your partner. If done at the wrong time, it can leave your side of the court exposed, giving your opponents an easy opportunity to win the point.

- **How to Poach Effectively Without Losing Position**:
    - To poach successfully, always maintain a ready position at the net. Keep your paddle up and stay on the balls of your feet, ready to move quickly. As soon as you see your opponent preparing for a weak shot, make your move toward the ball and execute the poach.

- After poaching, quickly reset your positioning to avoid leaving your side of the court exposed. This may involve backing up slightly or communicating with your partner to switch positions.

Effective Serving and Returning

In doubles pickleball, the serve and return of serve are critical elements of the game. A well-placed serve or return can set the tone for the rally and give you the upper hand.

- **Serving Strategies in Doubles**:
    - In doubles, the goal of the serve is to put your opponents on the defensive. A deep, well-placed serve can push them back toward the baseline, giving you more time to approach the net and control the kitchen line.
    - Avoid hitting short serves, as these give your opponents the opportunity to step in and attack. Instead, focus on deep, consistent serves that force your opponents to hit from less advantageous position.

- **Returning Serve in Doubles**:
    - The return of serve is equally important in doubles. Your primary objective is to return the serve deep into your opponent's court, keeping them back and preventing them from approaching the net too quickly.
    - After hitting the return, immediately move toward the kitchen line. This positioning allows you and your partner to take control of the net and puts pressure on your opponents to make a more difficult third shot.

Handling Fast Exchanges at the Net

In doubles pickleball, fast exchanges at the net are common, especially during volleys. These exchange require quick reflexes and the ability to read your opponent's movements.

- **Staying Low and Ready**:
    - To handle fast volleys, always stay in a low, athletic stance with your knees bent and your paddle in front of you. This ready position allows you to react quickly to shots on either side of your body.
    - Keep your paddle at chest height and avoid taking big swings at the ball. Instead, use short, controlled strokes to return fast volleys, focusing on placement rather than power.

- **Defusing Hard Shots**:

- When your opponents hit hard shots at you, the key is to absorb the pace of the ball. Rather than trying to match their power, focus on controlling the ball with soft hands and directing it to a more favorable position on the court.

- One effective tactic is to use a block volley, which involves simply placing the paddle in the ball's path to deflect the shot back over the net with minimal movement. This can take the pace off the ball and give you time to reset the rally.

Conclusion of Chapter 4

Doubles pickleball is all about teamwork, communication, and smart strategy. By mastering court positioning, perfecting dinking and poaching techniques, and learning to handle fast exchanges at the net, you and your partner can dominate your opponents. Remember, doubles play isn't just about individual skill—it's about working together as a cohesive unit to control the pace of the game and create winning opportunities.

Chapter 5: Mental Toughness and Game Preparation

Pickleball isn't just a game of physical skill—it's a mental battle as well. Maintaining focus, staying calm under pressure, and preparing effectively for matches are essential if you want to succeed, especially in competitive play. In this chapter, we will delve into how to develop mental toughness and the best ways to prepare for your games, both physically and mentally.

Mental Strength on the Court

Mental toughness is the ability to stay focused and composed, even when the pressure is on. Whether you're trailing in a match or facing a tough opponent, staying mentally sharp can make all the difference. Below are strategies to help strengthen your mental game.

- **Staying Focused and Positive**:
  - One of the keys to success in pickleball is staying focused, even when things aren't going your way. It's easy to get distracted by a bad shot or a few missed points, but dwelling on mistakes can quickly derail your game. Instead, learn to focus on the present moment and move on from errors.
  - Positive self-talk can help you stay in a good mental space during matches. Instead of criticizing yourself for a mistake, use encouraging language like, "I'll get the next one," or "Stay focused." This positive reinforcement will keep you motivated and prevent negative emotions from taking over.

- **Managing Pressure and Fatigue**:
  - Pressure can be your worst enemy on the court. Whether it's the final point of a close game or a critical moment in a tournament, the pressure can cause even the most

experienced players to lose focus. To manage pressure, try using breathing techniques take deep breaths between points to calm your mind and refocus.

- o Fatigue can also impact your mental sharpness. When you're tired, it's easy to lose focus and make poor decisions. To combat this, improve your endurance with off-court conditioning and develop the mental stamina to push through tough moments when fatigue sets in.

- **Developing a Growth Mindset**:

  - o In pickleball, as in any sport, losing is part of the game. The way you respond to losses can shape your future performance. Developing a **growth mindset** means viewing loss not as failures but as opportunities to learn and improve.

  - o After a tough match, reflect on what went wrong and how you can improve. Did you struggle with a particular type of shot? Were there moments where you lost focus? Use these experiences to grow as a player, rather than letting them discourage you.

Mental Strategies for Managing Different Match Scenarios

Different match situations require different mental approaches. Here are some ways to handle common scenarios you'll encounter on the pickleball court.

- **Playing From Behind**:

  - o When you're trailing in a match, it's easy to feel the pressure mounting. The key to coming back is to stay calm and focused. Avoid taking unnecessary risks in an attempt score quick points—stay patient and play your game.

  - o Break the game down into small goals, like winning the next point or getting your serve back. This helps keep you from feeling overwhelmed by the score and allows you to focus on one point at a time.

- **Holding Onto a Lead**:

  - o When you're ahead in a match, it's tempting to relax and let your guard down. However, this is often when players lose focus and allow their opponents to catch up. Even with a comfortable lead, stay focused on your strategy and don't start playing too conservatively.

  - o Avoid the mindset of "just getting the game over with." Keep playing the same aggressive or controlled style that got you the lead in the first place. Closing out games requires mental toughness and the ability to finish strong.

- **Handling Long Rallies**:

  - o Long rallies can be physically and mentally exhausting. During these moments, it's important to stay patient and avoid going for risky, low-percentage shots just to end the rally. Keep your focus on consistency and outlasting your opponent.

- o Mentally, remind yourself that a long rally is an opportunity to wear your opponent down, especially if they are less conditioned than you. Use these rallies to your advantage by staying composed and sticking to high-percentage shots.

ysical Preparation

addition to mental preparation, physical readiness is crucial for pickleball success. By improving your erall fitness, agility, and strength, you can enhance your performance on the court and minimize the k of injury.

- **Key Exercises to Improve Agility and Endurance**:
  - o **Agility Drills**: Agility is vital in pickleball, as you need to move quickly in all directions. Lateral shuffles, cone drills, and ladder drills can improve your foot speed and reaction time, allowing you to cover more ground on the court.
  - o **Endurance Training**: Pickleball matches can be long and physically demanding. Incorporating endurance exercises like jogging, swimming, or cycling will help build your cardiovascular fitness, enabling you to last longer on the court without getting fatigued.
  - o **Strength Training**: Building strength, especially in your legs and core, can improve your balance and power. Exercises like squats, lunges, and planks are great for building the necessary strength to stay strong during rallies.

- **Warm-Up Drills for Optimal Performance**:
  - o Warming up before a match is essential for preventing injuries and ensuring that you start the game feeling fresh and ready to move. A proper warm-up should include both dynamic stretches and light cardio exercises.
  - o Start with simple movements like arm circles, leg swings, and high knees to get your muscles activated. Follow this with a few minutes of light jogging or jumping jacks to increase your heart rate. Finally, practice a few short sprints or lateral shuffles to mimic the movements you'll be making during the game.

e-Match Routine and Preparation

tablishing a pre-match routine can help calm your nerves, get you mentally focused, and ensure u're physically ready to play your best. Here are some tips for creating an effective pre-match routine.

- **Mental Visualization**:
  - o Before stepping on the court, take a few moments to mentally visualize your game plan. Picture yourself executing key shots, moving efficiently on the court, and maintaining your focus throughout the match. Visualization can help you build confidence and reduce anxiety.

- Visualize potential challenges as well, such as how you will respond to pressure or adversity during the match. Mentally rehearsing these situations will prepare you to stay composed when they happen in real-time.

- **Setting Goals for the Match**:

  - Set specific, actionable goals for your match. These can be performance-related goals, such as improving your serve consistency or controlling the kitchen line more effectively. Focusing on these goals will help you stay present during the match and prevent distractions.

  - Avoid setting goals solely based on winning or losing. Instead, focus on aspects of your performance that are within your control. For example, "I will focus on making 80% of my serves" or "I will stay low and ready at the kitchen line."

Understanding Your Opponents

In pickleball, understanding your opponent's strengths and weaknesses can give you a significant advantage. Learning to "read" your opponent and adapt your strategy accordingly is a key skill for winning matches.

- **How to Analyze Your Opponent's Weaknesses**:

  - During the warm-up or early in the match, pay attention to your opponent's tendencies. Do they have a weaker backhand? Do they struggle with certain types of shots, like lobs or dinks? Identifying these weaknesses will help you target them during the match.

  - Also, observe their footwork and positioning. Are they slower to move laterally? Do they frequently get caught out of position? By noticing these patterns, you can adjust your strategy to exploit their vulnerabilities.

- **Adapting Your Gameplan Mid-Game**:

  - Being able to adapt your strategy during a match is a hallmark of a great pickleball player. If your original game plan isn't working, don't hesitate to make adjustments. For example, if your opponent is handling your deep shots with ease, try mixing in softer shots or dinks to change the pace.

  - Flexibility is key. Some players are very strong in one area but weak in others. The best players know how to shift their tactics to take advantage of whatever weaknesses their opponent reveals during the match.

Post-Game Reflection and Improvement

Improving in pickleball requires more than just practice—it also involves reflecting on your performance after each match. By analyzing what went well and where you struggled, you can make adjustments and continue to improve your game.

- **Analyzing Your Performance**:
    - After each game, take a few minutes to think about what worked and what didn't. Did you stick to your game plan? Were there specific shots or strategies that were particularly effective? Were there moments where you lost focus or made unforced errors?
    - Write down your thoughts, so you can refer back to them before your next match. Keeping a journal of your progress will help you identify patterns in your play and track your improvement over time.
- **Adjusting Your Training Based on Your Matches**:
    - Use your post-game reflections to inform your training. If you found that your backhand was weak during a match, focus on improving that shot in your next practice session. Similarly, if you struggled with endurance, incorporate more cardio training into your routine.
    - Every match is an opportunity to learn and grow. By consistently reflecting on your performance and adjusting your training accordingly, you'll become a more well-rounded and competitive player.

Conclusion of Chapter 5

Mental toughness and proper preparation are essential components of success in pickleball. By developing a strong mental game, staying physically fit, and preparing effectively for each match, you'll give yourself the best chance to perform at your highest level. Remember, the mental aspect of pickleball is just as important as the physical, and mastering both will make you a more formidable opponent on the court.

Chapter 6: Drills for Skill Improvement

To become a great pickleball player, consistent practice is key. Drills allow you to refine your technique, improve your reaction time, and develop muscle memory for critical shots. In this chapter, we will explore a variety of drills tailored to different aspects of the game, including dinking, serving, footwork, and doubles coordination. Whether you're a beginner looking to build your fundamentals or an experienced player aiming to fine-tune advanced techniques, these drills will help you elevate your game.

Dinking Drills

The dink is one of the most important shots in pickleball, especially in doubles play. Mastering dinking will allow you to control the pace of the game and force your opponents into making mistakes. These drills will help you improve your consistency, touch, and accuracy when dinking.

- **Dink Consistency Drill**:
    - **Objective**: Build consistency in dinking while keeping the ball low over the net.
    - **How to Perform**: Stand at the kitchen line and practice hitting soft dinks back and forth with a partner. Focus on keeping the ball as low as possible, landing it in your opponent's kitchen. Try to complete as many consecutive dinks as you can without missing. Start with 20 consecutive dinks and gradually increase the number as you improve.
    - **Key Focus**: Control, soft hands, and patience.

- **Crosscourt Dink Drill**:
    - **Objective**: Improve accuracy and the ability to hit crosscourt dinks.
    - **How to Perform**: Stand diagonally across from your partner at the kitchen line. Practice hitting crosscourt dinks, aiming for the far corner of your opponent's kitchen. This drill helps with accuracy and forces you to hit longer, softer shots that require touch.
    - **Key Focus**: Aiming for specific targets, controlling the length and arc of the dink.

- **Dink to Attack Drill**:
    - **Objective**: Learn when to transition from dinking to attacking.
    - **How to Perform**: Engage in a regular dinking rally with your partner. One player will suddenly hit a higher or weaker dink, simulating an opponent's mistake. The other player must then capitalize on this by attacking with a volley or smash. The goal is to practice transitioning smoothly from soft dinks to aggressive shots.
    - **Key Focus**: Recognizing attack opportunities and switching gears from defense to offense.

Serving Drills

A consistent and well-placed serve can set the tone for each rally. These drills will help you improve your serve's accuracy, power, and placement, giving you an advantage right from the start of the point.

- **Deep Serve Drill**:
    - **Objective**: Develop consistency in hitting deep serves that push your opponent back.
    - **How to Perform**: Stand behind the baseline and practice serving to different areas of the court. Focus on getting the ball to land close to your opponent's baseline. Set

targets (like cones) near the baseline and aim to hit the targets. Track your accuracy over time.

- ○ **Key Focus**: Depth, accuracy, and consistency.

- **Serve Placement Drill**:

  - ○ **Objective**: Learn to place your serve effectively to put your opponent in difficult positions.

  - ○ **How to Perform**: Divide your opponent's service box into zones (e.g., left, right, center). Serve 10 balls to each zone, focusing on accuracy and control. Alternate between different zones during your serves to keep your opponent guessing. This will also help you build a more versatile serve.

  - ○ **Key Focus**: Accuracy and ability to change up the placement of the serve.

- **Spin Serve Drill**:

  - ○ **Objective**: Practice adding spin to your serve to make it more difficult for opponents to return.

  - ○ **How to Perform**: Use a topspin or slice motion when serving to impart spin on the ball. Practice hitting spin serves to different zones on the court. Notice how the ball reacts when it bounces and adjust your spin technique to make the serve harder to return.

  - ○ **Key Focus**: Spin control and understanding how spin affects ball trajectory.

ootwork Drills

ood footwork is the foundation of strong pickleball play. These drills will improve your movement on e court, allowing you to reach the ball more efficiently and maintain balance during rallies.

- **Lateral Shuffle Drill**:

  - ○ **Objective**: Improve lateral movement and agility for better court coverage.

  - ○ **How to Perform**: Stand at the baseline and shuffle from one sideline to the other, staying low and balanced. Once you reach the opposite sideline, shuffle back. As you get better, increase your speed while maintaining control. You can also add a paddle and ball, hitting a soft shot at each sideline before shuffling to the other side.

  - ○ **Key Focus**: Lateral speed, balance, and foot positioning.

- **Split-Step Reaction Drill**:

  - ○ **Objective**: Develop the split-step technique for quick reactions to your opponent's shots.

  - ○ **How to Perform**: Have a partner feed balls to different areas of the court. Before each shot, perform a split-step (a small hop to get into a balanced, ready position) to prepare yourself for movement. This drill will improve your ability to react quickly and get to the ball.

- o **Key Focus**: Timing of the split-step and quick reactions.

- **Cone Drill for Court Coverage**:

  - o **Objective**: Practice covering the entire court with efficient footwork.

  - o **How to Perform**: Place cones at different points on the court (e.g., baseline corners, kitchen line, center). Move between the cones as quickly as possible, touching each cone before moving to the next. This drill simulates the quick changes in direction required during a game.

  - o **Key Focus**: Agility, speed, and proper movement patterns.

Doubles Coordination Drills

Doubles play requires seamless coordination with your partner. These drills focus on improving teamwork, communication, and court positioning during doubles matches.

- **Side-by-Side Movement Drill**:

  - o **Objective**: Improve coordination and movement with your partner.

  - o **How to Perform**: Stand side by side with your partner at the kitchen line. Have a coach or partner feed balls randomly to different areas of the court. Both you and your partner should move together, covering the court while staying aligned. The goal is to move as a unit and prevent any gaps between you.

  - o **Key Focus**: Synchronizing movement and maintaining proper spacing with your partner

- **Third Shot Drop Drill**:

  - o **Objective**: Practice executing the third shot drop with your partner to gain control of the net.

  - o **How to Perform**: One player serves, and the receiver hits a return shot deep into the court. The server's partner should then execute a third shot drop, aiming to land the ball softly in the opponent's kitchen. After the third shot drop, both players should move up to the kitchen line. This drill helps build confidence in using the third shot drop to transition to the net.

  - o **Key Focus**: Mastering the third shot drop and effective net transitions.

- **Crosscourt Rally Drill**:

  - o **Objective**: Improve crosscourt rally coordination with your partner.

  - o **How to Perform**: Engage in a crosscourt rally with your partner, focusing on consistency and accuracy. The goal is to keep the ball in play as long as possible while hitting to your partner's forehand or backhand side. This drill helps improve placement and control, and it strengthens the chemistry between you and your partner.

- o **Key Focus**: Crosscourt accuracy, rally endurance, and communication.

efensive Drills

efense is a crucial part of pickleball, especially when you're under pressure. These drills will help you velop the ability to reset the point and defend against aggressive opponents.

- **Resetting the Point Drill**:
  - o **Objective**: Learn how to reset the rally when you're on the defensive.
  - o **How to Perform**: Have a partner hit hard, fast shots toward you while you are positioned at the baseline or midcourt. Your goal is to reset the point by hitting soft, controlled shots that land in your opponent's kitchen, allowing you to transition to the net. Practice keeping the ball low to neutralize your opponent's advantage.
  - o **Key Focus**: Controlled defense, soft hands, and neutralizing your opponent's attack.
- **Blocking Drill**:
  - o **Objective**: Practice blocking fast-paced volleys or smashes at the net.
  - o **How to Perform**: Stand at the kitchen line while your partner hits aggressive volleys or smashes at you. Instead of returning the ball with power, practice blocking the shot by simply absorbing its energy with your paddle and directing it back over the net softly. This drill improves your ability to handle fast shots without losing control.
  - o **Key Focus**: Soft blocking, paddle control, and defensive composure.

onclusion of Chapter 6

acticing these drills consistently will help you develop the key skills necessary for both singles and ubles pickleball. Whether you're working on your dinks, serves, or footwork, drills are essential for proving your technique and building confidence in your game. Remember, the more time you spend fining your skills off the court, the more successful you'll be when it comes time to compete. corporate these drills into your regular practice sessions, and watch your pickleball performance soar.

onclusion

ckleball is a sport that combines physical skill, mental acuity, and strategic thinking, making it a game at can be enjoyed by players of all ages and levels. Throughout this guide, we've explored the essential les, techniques, strategies, and drills that will help you master the game, whether you're playing singles or doubles. However, this journey doesn't end with understanding the basics—it's a continuous process of learning, practicing, and refining your abilities to reach new heights on the court.

Recap of Core Strategies

- **Master the Fundamentals**: Success in pickleball begins with a solid foundation. Whether you're working on your serve, dinking technique, or court positioning, mastering the basic mechanics the game is the first step to becoming a better player. The more comfortable you are with the fundamentals, the more naturally advanced strategies and techniques will come.

- **Adapt and Evolve Your Game**: Every game and opponent is different, and the key to winning is your ability to adapt. Pay attention to your opponent's weaknesses, observe the flow of the match, and don't hesitate to switch up your tactics when necessary. Flexibility is one of the most important traits of a skilled pickleball player.

- **Communicate and Coordinate**: In doubles play, effective communication with your partner is essential. Always be in sync with your partner's movements, and make sure to support each other throughout the match. Developing this coordination will allow you to work as a team and overcome even the toughest opponents.

- **Focus on Mental Toughness**: Pickleball is as much a mental game as a physical one. Whether you're facing a challenging opponent or coming back from a deficit, staying focused, composed and positive will keep you in control. Develop mental strategies to manage pressure, stay motivated, and turn challenges into opportunities for growth.

- **Consistency and Practice**: Like any sport, the more you practice, the better you'll become. Consistent practice using drills designed to target specific skills—such as footwork, serving, and defense—will improve your game over time. Dedicate time to mastering the core shots and movements, and you'll find that your confidence and performance will grow.

How to Continue Improving Your Pickleball Game

Improvement in pickleball is an ongoing process. Here are some ways to continue progressing and refining your skills:

- **Play Regularly**: The best way to improve is to play as often as possible. Join local clubs, participate in open-play sessions, and take part in tournaments to challenge yourself against different types of opponents. The more you play, the more you'll experience various playing styles and strategies.

- **Stay Active in the Pickleball Community**: Pickleball has a thriving community, with local clubs, leagues, and social events that provide opportunities to connect with other players. Engage with this community to stay motivated, learn from more experienced players, and build lasting relationships.

- **Study Your Matches**: After every match or practice session, take time to reflect on your performance. What worked well, and where did you struggle? Analyze your strengths and weaknesses, and create a plan to work on the areas that need improvement. This reflective practice is key to long-term growth.

- **Work on Conditioning**: Physical fitness plays a huge role in pickleball. Staying in shape will improve your endurance, speed, and agility on the court. Incorporate regular cardio, strength training, and flexibility exercises into your routine to ensure that you can perform at your best in every match.

- **Continue Learning**: Never stop learning. Watch instructional videos, attend pickleball clinics, and study the strategies of top players to expand your knowledge. The more you learn, the more adaptable and versatile you'll become.

Embrace the Joy of the Game

While becoming a skilled pickleball player is important, it's equally crucial to enjoy the process. Pickleball is a sport that brings people together and fosters a sense of community and camaraderie. Whether you're playing competitively or just for fun, always take the time to appreciate the joy of the game.

Remember, it's not just about winning—it's about improving, enjoying the experience, and connecting with others. Whether you're spending an afternoon playing with friends, honing your skills at a practice session, or competing in a tournament, always keep the fun and excitement of pickleball in mind.

The Future of Your Pickleball Journey

As you continue your pickleball journey, keep striving to challenge yourself and push your limits. Set personal goals, track your progress, and celebrate your achievements, no matter how small they may seem. Whether you're aiming to master a new shot, win a local tournament, or simply improve your consistency, every step forward is a testament to your dedication and love for the game.

Remember, the more time you invest in your pickleball skills, the more you'll get out of it. Stay curious, stay motivated, and, most importantly, keep playing!

Final Words

Pickleball is an incredible sport that offers fun, fitness, and friendship, and there's always something new to learn. With the knowledge and strategies outlined in this guide, you're now equipped to take your game to the next level. Keep practicing, stay patient with your progress, and enjoy every moment you spend on the court. Whether you're playing for competition or recreation, pickleball is a game that will reward your efforts and provide you with endless opportunities for growth and enjoyment.

Here's to your continued success and improvement—see you on the pickleball court!

Made in the USA
Monee, IL
27 December 2024

75456424R00017